Poetic Ballets
of my Mind

PHYLLIS KWAN

Poetic Ballets of My Mind
by
Phyllis Kwan

Published by:
In Our Words Inc.
www.inourwords.ca

Illustrations "High Heels" and "Falling Leaves"
by Susan E. Blanchard

Editor: Cheryl Antao-Xavier

Book design: Shirley Aguinaldo

Author's photo: Orchid Photography

Library and Archives Canada Cataloguing in Publication

Kwan, Phyllis, author
    Poetic ballets of my mind / Phyllis Kwan.

Poems.
ISBN 978-1-926926-59-9 (paperback).

ISBN 978-1-926926-60-5 (hardcover)

    I. Title.

PS8621.W35P63 2016   C811'.6   C2016-900704-9

All Rights Reserved. Copyright © Phyllis Kwan, 2016.
The author retains all rights to the contents of this book.
Brief quotes may be used with source credit.
Book design © In Our Words Inc.

"With heaven and earth contained in your head/ nothing escapes the pen in your hand."[1]

- Lu Ji, (famous third century Chinese poet)

---

1 Tony Barnstone and Chou Ping, *The Anchor Book of Chinese Poetry*, Anchor Books—a division of Random House Inc., and in Canada by Random House of Canada Limited, Toronto. February, 2005. Pg. 66

INTRODUCTION

I have always loved the English language. Even growing up as an ethnic Chinese girl in Trinidad, I took to English literature like a duck to water. I loved reading poetry and novels.

When I got married in 1978, life got in the way with work and family. I had little time to read for pleasure. From 1998 to 2014, I wrote perhaps fifteen poems in total. Early in 2015, I met a cousin, Jason, who introduced me to the works of Pablo Neruda, a Nobel Prize winner in literature. As I read Neruda's famous poems, images instantly sprang to mind. One result is my poem "The Conqueror," of which I am especially proud.

In 2006, when my beloved father, Edward Ayoung-Chee died, I was stricken with grief. However, I have always felt enveloped by my father's love even after his death. So I know that he will be with me until the day I die. I carry him in my heart. Late one night, almost six years after he passed, I felt compelled to write a poem about his final days. I was already determined to write a book to tell the world how wonderful he was as a man and a parent. While he was in palliative care, I showed my father in every way that I could that I loved him with all my heart. I have included a tribute to him in this collection.

Throughout my life, I have been the eternal optimist in my family, the perennial romantic, and the sentimental one. I truly believe in LOVE and that it makes the world a better place. The great love stories in literature and cinema have a deep impact on me and on my imagination. Some of my favourite movies are *Casablanca*, *The Sound of Music*, *It's A Wonderful Life*, *Ghost*, *The English Patient*, *Bridges of Madison County*, *Kate and Leopold*, *The Notebook*, *The Princess Bride*, and *Avatar*. In this collection, I have alluded to the thoughts and movies that inspired some of my poems.

In a couple of instances in my book, I must claim poetic license. To achieve the desired effect and against the advice of my editor, I insisted that my original words be used instead of her editorial suggestions. Thank you, Cheryl, for your diligence and professionalism.

I would like to acknowledge my husband and my family for their love and support. A special thanks to my cousin Jason Chee-Hing, and my dear friend Susan E. Blanchard, for their encouragement and support.

Phyllis Kwan

TABLE OF CONTENTS

A Tribute To Love 9
    Ode To My Father 10
    My Love, My Life's Partner 13
    Sunshine 14
    The Conqueror 15
    Unfulfilled Love 16
    Temptation 17
    Remember Me 18
    Dimples 20
    Hurting 21
    Images 22

Ballet Of The Palms 23
    Ballet Of The Palms 25
    Goedemorgen, Aruba 26

Reflections 27
    Reflections 28
    The Waterfront 29
    Do You Love Me Still? 30
    My Man Don't Dance 31
    First Kiss 32
    Grow Old With Me, My Love 34
    Friendship 35
    What Is Important 36
    Take It In Stride 38
    Childlike Innocence 39

    Oh, To Be In Love Again 40
    My Little Liam 41
    Desolate 42
    The Joy In Knowing You 44
    Such A Small Thing 45
    My Day In The Sun 46
    Full Moon 47
    Never Forgotten 48
    Survival 49
    In Spite Of Myself 50
    If I Were Your Woman 51
    Falling Leaves 52
    Are You Dead? 54
    I Remember 55
    Summer Picnic 56
    The Magic Of Movies 57
    My Garden 58
    My Platonic Friend 59
    Accustomed To You 62
    You Know Me Well 63
    Good Neighbour 64
    High Heels 65
    Fight 66
    Perfect Life 67

Reclaiming My Heritage 69
    Reclaiming My Heritage 70

Most of the poems in this section "A Tribute to Love" were written between 1998 and 2014. I included these earlier poems to demonstrate my evolution as a writer and a poet. The innocence and naïveté of my younger years are somewhat evident in my style of writing in this period.

The more recent poems were written with an ease and creative style that has developed considerably with experience. I have also found that my vision and viewpoint have mellowed, and I am more patient, tolerant, understanding, and hopefully wiser, at this stage in my life. I know that my writing today reflects that maturity.

A Tribute to Love

ODE TO MY FATHER
(a tribute to Edward Ayoung-Chee)

I see you lying there
A shadow of your former self
There is a knot in my chest
My heart aches painfully.

I sense your fear
I feel your discomfort
This is not how you are used to being seen
This is not how you wish to be remembered.

We have to pull together
We have to bear the shock and be there for you
We need to be strong and work together
We have to make you as comfortable as we can.

You are my wise hero, my first love
You are so tall and handsome, strong, righteous and fair
You are my father, and in my eyes
You are the perfect man.

Now here you are in your golden years
Struck down by illness and disease
But still the man I have loved from infancy
Still the man I adore.

Our culture suggests that distance be kept
And emotions be held at bay
No embarrassing displays, please
So that the journey to heaven be eased.

But customs be damned for they are absurd!
Heartless suggestions are cruel and weird
Thoughtless comments wound you deeply and surely
Taking away hurtful barbs lets me live my life purely.

I could see your thankfulness in your eyes
As I lambaste those who hurt and wound you
They are greedy and crude and do not love you as I do
They never would and never could.

And that love for you I will not hide
Most especially in these your final days
I want the world to know the love and respect
I hold in my heart for you.

I want to disclose all to you
I want to hold you so that you are sure
That you were never loved more
That your memory will always endure.

I wish to stroke away your pain and fear
I wish to do all and be all you need
And when I do and see you smile
All the sacrifices seem so worthwhile.

We know that you are at death's door
And that you now fear no more
We feel your pride in us, your six girls
We see the love in your eyes.

Daddy, I will adore you all the days of my life
I will treasure memories of a wonderful childhood
You, my dearest father, made it all possible
Thank you, Dad, for everything.

Dad, may you rest in peace with a heart that's content
Comfortable and secure in our care
I will never forget the light in your eyes
And your happiness that shone from within, at the end.

God bless and keep you forever and forever
Adieu, sweet man, whom I call father
Adieu, my dear Edward, till we meet again
Adieu, my beloved father, my dear friend.

'Ode to My Father' was written with all the love in my heart for a father whom I adored. My dad was generous and loving to his daughters, and I thank him from the bottom of my heart for the wonderful childhood I enjoyed and the lovely life I had while living at home. When I got married and had my own family, I vowed to provide a good life for my children and to create happy memories for them, as happy as the memories my father created for me.

I love you, Daddy, and I always will.

MY LOVE, MY LIFE'S PARTNER
(my very first poem – August, 1998)

You are my life's partner
and the center of my world
All that I strive for is
for you, our boy and our girl.

You have made me so happy
I am triply blessed
All I can think of is our family
And your happiness.

Your goodness, truth and simplicity
are all very rare to find
and on this day, my vows to you
I will always keep in mind.

I will love you, honour you, cherish you
and be forever by your side
all the days of my life
my love, my husband, my darling Steve.

SUNSHINE

Sunshine, it is warm and golden
Sunshine, it creates and maintains life
Sunshine, it is beautiful and bright
Sunshine, it makes me happy
Sunshine, it takes away the darkness
Sunshine, it permeates my being
Sunshine, it is good.
Andrew, my son—*You are my Sunshine.*

THE CONQUEROR

Body of a man, broad shoulders, sculpted chest,
chiselled buttocks, thighs of thunder
Looming above, a conqueror ready to vanquish and plunder
Mighty and impervious in your arrogance
Sensing a weak and easy prey, you are poised for victory
My soft pliant body cradles your hardness
My round white thighs cushion your blows
As you pound my quivering flesh
As you lower yourself deep in my embrace.

Alone like the pyramids in the desert,
Aloof and isolated, you stand magnificent
King of all you observe as far as the eye could see
When our paths crossed, pulsating waves pounded
You set out to defeat and master all in your path
Wishing to slake your thirst momentarily
And to silence the growl of your lustful loins
Little did you know you would be enslaved.

Your sword thrusts deep within
Your metal cleaves through brush drawing blood
Your eyes widen yet still you plunder until you shudder
The creamy river flows unbridled and unchecked
Your thirst is slaked, your hunger appeased for the hour
Until the constant pangs attack yet again, golden warrior
Until you once again seek
The body of a woman.

Who is mightier now, my lord?
Which of us is the vanquished, which one the conqueror?

UNFULFILLED LOVE

You are a kindred spirit
You touch my soul like no-one else ever has.
You hear me call you
Yet I have not uttered a sound.
I can sense your presence
Yet my eyes have not yet seen you.
Our bodies have never intertwined
But our minds and souls have made love
Passionately …
Endlessly.

You are my love from another life
And destiny has decreed
Our paths cross once again.
You are my soulmate
I tried to deny you
But it was futile.
You are the wiser one
You knew and recognized what was between us
Instinctively …
Truthfully.

TEMPTATION

Should I beg you for fulfillment
Please, please deny me
Should I crave your attentions
Please, please ignore me
Resist all my charms and wiles
For to surrender would only lead to
My destruction.

You have to be the strong one
I am weak-kneed at your magnificence
I want to sink my teeth into your shoulders
Feel your heartbeat pounding against mine
Let thundering waves of pleasure wash over us
As you spiral us both to ecstasy.

But after the moment has passed
I will live my life in regret and guilt
… and in constant need of you.
So, don't tempt me
Please, please don't tempt me
Don't tempt me, my love
If I give myself to you completely
I will be lost forever.

REMEMBER ME

Remember me, my beloved
When I am no longer with you
Not with sadness, nor with pain
But with pleasure and happiness true.

Your happiness may be laced with regret
Your pleasure tinged with slight remorse
Because I left you surely but unwillingly
But in truth, there was no other recourse.

You brought me all manner of ecstasy
You unleashed my innocent heart
And I will always remember how you loved me
We'll forever be one being, even if we're apart.

My honour binds me to another
Motherhood and duty hold me fast
Goodness and high ideals are all I knew
And my future is forged by my past.

In your arms, I find heaven on earth
I soar in your embrace to the sky
You destroy all my fears and inhibitions
I love you completely, yet I don't know why.

Your kisses take my breath away
Your gaze and touch mesmerize
I don't recognize the woman I've become
Yet she is me, in truth, I see her in your eyes.

I derive such happiness just looking at you
To be in your company is pure bliss
Your handsome face, devil eyes, virile body
Are simple joys that I will sorely miss.

But you say we're still together
That we have not severed our ties
But because I know who, how, and what I am
I see where our future truly lies.

Even as I am sated with your lovemaking
Aglow with contentment in your bed
When I ponder our future together
My soul begins to fill with dread.

I am afraid of having to leave you
I am afraid I will cause you much pain
I know my heart will never forget you
I know I will never love like this again.

But before our love is discovered
And havoc is wreaked on innocent lives
I do not wish to harm my family
That is why I must sever our ties.

I know someday I must leave you
With memories of brandy and a full moon
My heart will break at our parting
Not just yet, my love, but soon… too soon!!

This poem was inspired by the movie Bridges of Madison County, *starring Clint Eastwood and Meryl Streep. It was based on a true story. Also, inspirational was the movie* Shakespeare in Love.

DIMPLES

I love dimples.

Carved into your cheeks
One on each side
The left holds mirth
And the right holds mischief.

The sight of them is a nice surprise
As they deepen and reveal themselves
They send my weary spirits soaring
And happiness fills the air.

I love to see you smile
Because you elicit mine in return.

HURTING

It hurts to know that you are ill
That there's a chance you may leave
It hurts to think perhaps you'll not be around
And the very thought makes me grieve.

You will miss the children growing up
You will miss the sunlight on your face
You won't hear me calling you
This world will become a dreary place.

I am afraid of losing more loved ones
Mother, nephew, childhood friend
I pray, dear God, that He spares you
So that our relationship never ends.

Know that you are always in my heart
Know that you cannot ever be replaced
Know that I will always love you
I will always remember your lovely face.

'Hurting' was written in the year I learned that my nephew and a childhood friend were diagnosed with cancer.

IMAGES

tossing and turning
wishing and yearning
teasing and pleasing
wanting and burning

writhing and riding
below and above you
straddling and spooning
digging my nails into you

such are the illicit images
that flutter through my mind
skimming unbidden
and wantonly unkind

torturing myself with images
of what could possibly be
if only you loved me and
we were both free

muscled, chiselled, and with a heart of gold
you are sensitive, intelligent, masterful, bold
but what keeps me waxing lyrically
is the hope that we will love one another
purely platonically

Ballet of the Palms

*At the Mira Sol Lounge watching the palm trees dance their ballet in the wind
—photo Phyllis Kwan.*

*Palm Beach, Aruba
where the author was inspired on her walks
to write "Goedemorgen, Aruba"*

BALLET OF THE PALMS

Alone, I nestle in my soft armchair
A refreshing gin and tonic in hand
The waitress brings a bowl of nuts
I relax, sinking deeply into the bowels of my seat.

My senses slowly revive from the onslaught of life
And awaken to my idyllic surroundings
I drink in the indigo-blue night sky
Sprinkled with a handful of stars.

I smell the salty sea air
I hear the gurgling cadence of a waterfall
And before my very eyes
The palm trees begin to dance.

They are subject to their master, the wind
And oh, what a glorious wind it is
The trees bow, they sway, they splay
They dance with utmost grace and joy.

Their exuberance is infectious
They lack inhibition of any sort
They dance unfettered in pure glee
Totally oblivious and absolutely carefree.

Their limbs are slender and supple
Resilient and flirtatious
Their wispy fronds wave with abandon
As they obey the wind's every command.

What a beautiful sight it is to see
How I wish you were here with me
So our hearts are captivated in unison
By the enchanting ballet of the palms.

GOEDEMORGEN, ARUBA

It is a glorious day on Palm Beach
full of soft, warm sunshine and balmy breezes
I feel the soft caress of the sun on my face
And the breezes swirl around me playfully
It is early morning, the sky is a stunning blue
with puffy white marshmallow clouds high above.

A handful of people are walking on the pristine beach
Each one I pass smiles and says "good morning"
sometimes in Spanish, but mostly in English
If no words are exchanged
a smile or a nod suffices
to make me feel happy and content
to be on Palm Beach and *in this moment*
exchanging pleasantries
exchanging courtesies
with complete strangers.

It is a beautiful world on this "one happy island"
The land of aloe and the Divi tree is a lovely place to be
Joie de vivre is evident in this paradise where
I want to shout out with good cheer
"Goedemorgen, Aruba! I love it here."

Reflections

REFLECTIONS

Now and then, I like to look back
dwell on my past,
ponder on the present,
plan for my future.
Now and then, I reflect on my life.

I like to see where I have been
The mistakes I have made along the way
so I may learn from them.
I like to assess where I am now
my happiness and contentment
at this point of today
so that I can make changes if I must, if I may.

Life is too short to be lived in misery.
Though at times I must accept what must be.
But if I can make changes to be happy
in the now and for my tomorrows,
I know I must do so
quickly and decisively.

Henceforth I must plan for my tomorrow
so that when it becomes my today,
I can assess my life in its entirety
and "Yes, I'm happy" is what I will say.

THE WATERFRONT

You suggest we meet for coffee
You'd like to see me before I leave.
I mention that I am claustrophobic
That we should meet in a quiet, open space
And you suggest the waterfront.

I had no idea what to expect
So I was very pleasantly surprised.
The wide expanse was in no way confining
The view was panoramic, and the air refreshing.
I didn't expect to have as much fun as I did.
The night was velvety soft, warm and magical.

We shared our poetry over coffee and sandwiches
You surprised me with the gift of Pablo Neruda.
Sitting on a bench, chatting like old friends
Listening to music and dancing into the night
Was so much fun and exhilarating.

I felt so appreciated by you
So worthy of your care and consideration
Your attention to my comfort and pleasure
Shows your immense kindness.
I felt like a much younger version of myself
And it is a boon to have found such a friend in you.
Poetic soul that you are
You stimulate my mind and all of my senses.

DO YOU LOVE ME STILL?

I live each day moving in slow motion
Trying not to look back or dwell on our past
I am determined to live in the present, look to the future
And not live in regret for what is now lost.

I adored our adventures and untold pleasure
I realize that all things do change and end
I am thankful for the love we shared
And treasure our time together, dear friend.

Moving forward is the hardest thing
Because in my heart I love you still
But knowing I am not what you need
I release you; I must and I will.

But before I move ahead with my life
I need to know "Do you love me still?"
If you do, we'll meet in the next lifetime
And my beloved, it will be such a thrill.

Hopefully, when next we meet,
I won't be too early and you won't be too late.
Timing is everything, my sweet, and in our next life
You will be my Leopold and I will be your Kate.

Inspired by two movies: **Bridges of Madison County** *starring Meryl Streep and Clint Eastwood, and* Kate and Leopold *starring Meg Ryan and Hugh Jackman.*

MY MAN DON'T DANCE

He is stalwart and strong
A pillar of dependability
A powerhouse of responsibility
He stands firm in his beliefs
And will not compromise his principles
But my man don't dance.

He can be as gentle as a dove
As understanding as a shrink
He's great at making love
He stimulates my mind and makes me think
He is understanding and shrewd
But my man don't dance.

A handsome Adonis with the grace of a leopard
Muscled and sexy and smart to boot
He is never uncouth or overly loud
With a bearing that makes him noble and proud
I admire his charming ways and his sense of style
But my man don't dance.

It is enough that he sets my blood afire
I swoon when he hugs and kisses me
My world is full of all that is good
Whenever he is around
My happiness abounds.
But my man don't dance.

Who cares? Not me.
I don't really give a damn!
I'm just so glad that he's my man.

FIRST KISS

You lean in to kiss me
My heart starts to pound
I want to escape
But I am mesmerized
By the look in your eyes.

As you get closer to me
Your clean, fresh scent is so appealing
It wafts on the waves of your body heat
I inhale your heady masculinity.

Our lips touch with sweet gentleness
Your lips thin, firm and masterful
You increase your pressure on my yielding mouth
Involuntarily, my trembling lips part
And you plunder the softness within.

I am giddy with excitement
Dizzy and lightheaded in your arms
My whole world starts to spin
I feel as if I am floating above the universe
Nothing else matters but to be held in your arms.

Your kiss deepens and I am captivated
You masterfully invade my mouth
You run your tongue over my teeth
Our two breaths become one
You draw my heart out of me.

Then the duel playfully and lovingly begins.
Fencing artfully, you play with my tongue
You taste delicious and I savour your flavour

Then to my surprise, you gently nibble at my lips
I catch my breath and come up gasping for air
My knees are weak and they give way
I would fall if not for your strong embrace.

I hear your devilish chuckle
I see the sensual glint in your eyes
You know how much you affect me
And I can see in your beautifully, dreamy eyes
That I have a profound effect on you too.

How wonderful our first kiss was.
There is longing and a wish for more.
Your touch sets me afire and you taste so delicious
Your kiss is something I simply adore.
I hope you find me pleasing and enjoy kissing me
But it won't be as much as I enjoy kissing you.

GROW OLD WITH ME, MY LOVE

I watch while you sleep and wonder
How will you age in the years to come?
Will you lose all your teeth?
Will your hairline recede?
Will you develop a paunch?
Will your hair turn gray?
Will your fine physique sag?
Will your memory fade?
Will your intelligence wane?
All these questions come to mind.

But no matter what changes occur
You will still see the glimmer of love in my eyes
You will still see a smile linger on my lips
You will still hear my words of love for you
You will still feel the gentleness of my soft caress
You will still know in every word I say, in everything I do
That my love is forever—that my love is true.

And I will be glad to have you
Grow old with me, my love.

FRIENDSHIP

Come play with me and be my friend
And your joys and sorrows my ear I will lend
We will chant and sing and dance around
And in childish glee, fall to the ground.

As we grow up, I pledge to thee
Your greatest friend I will truly be
In times of need, in times of strife
I swear I will be your friend for life.

To you I will be a kindred spirit
My love for you has no end, has no limit
I will be there for you every step of the way
I will support and help you every single day.

I will console you in all your disappointments
And rejoice with you in all your accomplishments
People will be envious of me and you
Because our friendship will be steadfast and true.

I promise to comfort you in matters of the heart
My beloved friend, I hope we will never part
If you should hurt me, I will forgive you, dear friend
Because I am loyal, your true friend to the end.

For my best friend Susan Blanchard and dear friend Helen Orfanidis.

WHAT IS IMPORTANT

When I tell you something is important to me
And you dismiss it peremptorily
You undermine my importance and my integrity
You compromise my self-worth and self-esteem
Does that mean I am unimportant to you?

If you do not appreciate what's in my heart,
Or what I think and what I say to you
Or the information I share with you
How can you appreciate the woman I am?
How can you hold me in high esteem?

You belittle the significance of the things I tell you
You listen but don't hear my words
And because I'm not granted what I ask for
I ask again and again repeatedly
Then you call me controlling, a nag and a shrew.

I am tired of being unheard
Tired of being taken for granted
Tired of always giving and not getting in return
So I now give you due notice
I may just walk out that door.

Now will you believe me when I say it is important?
I do mean it is of paramount importance
If it wasn't meaningful, I would not say it was
Obviously, you still don't know me very well
And you don't recognize my worth.

Well, I am controlling because I am responsible
For my life and for my own happiness
I decide my actions so I may be happy
I will be in control of my life
I will walk away from you.

So when next I say it is important,
Mark my words and heed me well
You need me for your comfort and happiness
This I know with truth and conviction
I know I can survive on my own
But you will drown in an abyss of despair.

TAKE IT IN STRIDE

Through the good and bad
The 'happy' and 'sad'
Take it easy
Take it in stride.

Through the bad-mouthing
And the vicious gossiping
Be strong
Take it in stride.

When you don't see eye-to-eye
They call you a bitch
When you tell them your preference
They call you controlling

When they don't get their way
They call you manipulative
When you get angry
You're a shrew and they want to tame you.

"Don't sweat the small stuff"
Hold your head high with pride
Live your life for the greater good
And just take it all in stride.

CHILDLIKE INNOCENCE

Often as a child, when I walked home from school
I remember an overwhelming feeling of well-being
I looked up at the beautiful clear blue sky
With puffy white clouds sailing on by.

I would give thanks and praise for the beautiful day
Feeling that all of life was going my way
I would speak out loud in childlike innocence
"I am glad to be alive! Lord, I feel Your love every day."

I loved talking to our heavenly Father, our Almighty God
I thanked Him for giving us His only Son, Jesus Christ
I praised the Holy Spirit, Maker of heaven and earth
I thanked God for the blessings I have received from birth.

And God answered me in so many different ways
He made my life bountiful, joyful and gay
When I received His blessings, you'd hear me say
I know I am blessed each and every day!

Thank you, God, our Father in heaven.
Thank you, Jesus Christ, our Saviour and the Holy Spirit.
Thank you, Mother Mary of the Immaculate Conception
Thank you, angels and saints and all the souls in heaven.

Please grant us happiness and keep us safe.
Help us learn to love and respect each other.
Help us learn forgiveness. And grant us peace.
Amen.

OH, TO BE IN LOVE AGAIN

When I am in love
I feel oh so good!
I glisten and glow with happiness
The world is a wondrous place
I feel beautiful through and through
All because of your love for me
And my enduring love for you.

When I am in love
My feet have wings as I fly to you
I smile and people smile back at me
The rose has a sweeter scent
The sky is bluer, the grass is greener
Everything is better
Just because we are together.

When I am in love
There is nothing that I cannot do
I can scale the highest mountain peaks
I can sail the seven seas
I can build the Taj Mahal
I can jump over the CN Tower
The impossible suddenly becomes a possibility
All because of you and your love for me.

MY LITTLE LIAM

Utterly adorable, little toddler of mine
Beams of light from your eyes sparkle and shine
Your infectious chuckle, your roly-poly arms
Your thighs of thunder … are just some of your charms
Your wispy, light brown hair, your almond eyes
Your facial expressions make you appear so wise
Way beyond your tender age and our hearts you do capture
When I am with you, I am enthralled and enraptured
My little prince, my darling baby boy
You are my source of endless joy.

A little premature, you were three weeks early
With love and attention, you're now quite burly
Drinking six bottles of milk every day
Has its definite benefit and paves the way
For a baby boy with a healthy appetite
Bigger in stature and stronger in might
Yet you will never grow to be
Too big to sit on grandma's knee
What should we name you? Phillip or William?
Oh, I know my darling boy, we'll call you Liam!

DESOLATE

Can't eat
Can't sleep
Can't stop crying too
Can't stop my heart from breaking
Want to scream and explode in pain
Want to dive in front of a train.
Why did you have to go?

Used to call you at least three times a day
Used to write you always to say
Used to love you without reason or rhyme
Used to think about you all the time
Used to live for the times when we met
What happened to us ... did you forget?
Why did you have to go?

Tears run down my face, carving rivulets of pain
There's a knife twisting in my gut and I remain
Alone, lonely and hurting so
God, I wish the pain would go
There is no end to my pain in sight
No-one knows of my plight
Why did you have to go?

They say that time all wounds will heal
And that time even the memories will steal
But like a seasoned warrior, I will be scarred
And my memories of you can never be barred
My love is still strong, will be endless
Thoughts of you are relentless.
Why did you have to go?

You leave me desolate, empty and broken
Promises of love were mere words spoken.
Yet I would do it again, though it be in vain
Because the happiness outweighs the pain
I would be your lover, your woman, your wife
I would stay at your side in this journey of life.
Why did you have to go?

THE JOY IN KNOWING YOU

Calm as a windless day
you are serene and quiet
bringing peace to my heart
and there is joy in knowing you.

Right as rain, cultured and true
you are learned and erudite
wise as Solomon
and there is joy in knowing you.

Gentle as a lamb, strong as an ox
you are kind and charming too
straight as an arrow, sly as a fox
and there is joy in knowing you.

As pure as the driven snow
as sure as the day is long
I will always recall throughout my life
the joy I have found in knowing you.

SUCH A SMALL THING

a little gesture, like a phone call
such a small thing
has my heart beating fast
as if I have run a hundred miles

a text or an email from you
makes me feel warm and special
I read and re-read your messages
as they tell me you thought of me

a little kind and caring act
like making dinner for just us two
is a measure of my value and worth
I feel as if I am a Queen to you

a little smile
on your lips
meant only for me
tells me how much you care

a little glint in your eyes
when you look at me
shows how much you appreciate
and enjoy my company

these little things mean so much
they validate me and touch my heart
they help me appreciate the man you are
your kindness sets you a world apart

these little things show I am very blessed
to have you in my life is a boon to me
you are charming, gentle and kind
you are everything I could wish you to be.

MY DAY IN THE SUN

I am young and beautiful now
I hold you here in my arms
And know my dreams have come true
And that this is my day in the sun.

To know you love me as the air you breathe
To have you declare your undying need
To show this to me in all that you do
Is what makes this my day in the sun.

This ring you have given me today
Is a symbol of our enduring love
I vow to love you forever
I will always cherish my day in the sun.

FULL MOON

ethereal
majestic
mystical
almost spiritual

shimmering and glowing
ascending in the sky
like a golden goddess
sailing on high

perfect and round in your huge fullness
a glorious globe bursting with light
you are a wondrous celestial being
and truly, a most beauteous sight

inspiring poets and lovers all over the world
to gaze at you in silent repose
to sing your praise in ballads and songs
and pay you homage in rhyme and prose

full moon, magical moon
cast your spell upon my beloved
shine on him and shine on me
shine on us both simultaneously

touch his heart as you now touch mine
help him remember that long-forgotten time
when we frolicked in the grass and laughed and kissed
when we fell in love in a time of sheer bliss.

NEVER FORGOTTEN

Could I ever have forgotten in the fullness of time?
Could I lose the significance of what you brought to my life?
I doubt that even in a hundred lifetimes
That I will ever forget the remarkable man you are
You appeal to my romantic heart and
You awaken all of my dreams and all of my senses.

To see you is a delight to my eyes
A beautiful thing is a joy forever
To inhale you is an aromatic pleasure
I delight in your fresh, clean, masculine scent
To taste you is a delicious, intoxicating experience
Your lips are as sweet as the nectar of the gods.

To hear you is to delight in your voice
Your deep manly tones resonate in my soul
To feel your touch is pleasure beyond imagination
When we make love not just our bodies entwine
Our minds and our souls engage as well
We inspire each other to learn and grow
And we are better for having known and loved one other.

Oh, my darling, you could never be forgotten
I will remember you forever till the end of time
Even beyond death for a hundred lifetimes
I will search for you through all eternity
Knowing you are my one and only soulmate
Knowing you are my true love, my one destiny.

SURVIVAL

In intense pain and despair
with your heart aching, you ask
how do I survive the agony?
how do I continue to live?

You fix a smile on your face
numb your mind and heart
go through your routine
just survive, get through the day
then cry it out at night
when you are alone
and out of sight.

In time, your wounds will heal
the memory will slowly fade
a torturous, tedious, laborious process
but God makes us resilient
and eventually, things do get better.

You find the strength to go on
and your agony eases
you can breathe again
you can smile again
you can live again
once more.

IN SPITE OF MYSELF

Love me for who and what I am
Love me in spite of myself
See the heart of gold within
Overlook the human imperfections.

My wealth is my kind and generous nature
I live life with exuberance and deep appreciation
Never embarrassed to do a kind deed
Never ashamed to lend a helping hand.

I am good to others and expect the same from them
Taking pride in the things I say and do
Fully understanding the consequences of my actions
I am myself—I appreciate the person I am.

I see the human flaws and deficiencies in me
And strive to change and improve my character
I try to be honest with myself and admit my mistakes
And to learn from them and not repeat them.

I know filial piety, love and respect for family
I feel love and respect for my fellow man
Everyone has the freedom and right to be happy
And not everyone will think the way I do.

IF I WERE YOUR WOMAN

If I were your woman
And you were my lover
I would need no one else
You would need no other.

I would bear your sons and daughters
I would clean and cook for you
I would keep the romance stoked and burning
My love would be steadfast and true.

My active imagination may exasperate you
My headstrong ways may be hard to bear
I would strive to always amuse you
And in creative ways show you I care

I would live and give my life for you
Together we are complete, together we are whole
I will build you up and never tear you down
I will love you with all of my heart and soul.

FALLING LEAVES

falling autumn leaves
like my fallen dreams
blown and scattered
broken and tattered

harbinger of dreary days
bitter, biting winds whistle by
winter's breath is drawing near
my heart fills with dread and fear

how will I survive the frigid, lonely nights?
how will I live life on my own?
I have loved you for so many reasons
I have loved you for so many seasons

you leave me alone and in despair
my heart is broken, barren and bare
like the desolate trees, stripped and naked now
that await the heavy, wintry blanket of snow.

ARE YOU DEAD?

Silence
Emptiness
Nothingness
Desolation

Haven't heard a word from you
There have been no calls, emails or texts
Say something, all I know is that you're gone
Are you dead? Or are you still alive?

Thought we would always be friends
We had been friends before and much, much more
Why are you giving me the silent treatment?
Did I do something to alienate you or make you sore?

It would be nice to know that you are alive
It would be nice to know that you are happy now
I would be glad if you have moved on and are fine
I would be glad that your heart is not shattered like mine.

Silence says you do not care anymore
Emptiness is what I feel since you have gone
Nothingness is your gift to me on our special days too
Desolation is knowing that I am now dead to you.

I REMEMBER

I remember your dazzling smile
I remember your firm, masterful touch
I remember the glint in your eye
I remember the sweet times gone by

I love the way you arch an eyebrow
I love your bold, daring ways
I love how you scam and scheme
How you fulfill my every dream

The pleasure was seeing you every day
The pleasure was listening to all you say
The pleasure was when you held me in your arms
The pleasure was when I enjoyed all your charms

I remember how we laughed and played
I remember how we fought and made up
I remember all our adventures and all of the fun
I will always remember our days in the sun.

SUMMER PICNIC

Children running, shouting joyously
Splashing through the water sprinklers
Playing on swings and slides, they laugh infectiously
Their laughter delights as we picnic with family.

Freshly cooked food, all homemade and delicious
Lots of juice and water keep us hydrated
Soft ice cream is a must when the truck goes by
Delicious treats that are simply yummy.

Seated on blankets, the women chat and gossip
While the men play cards at the picnic tables
Everyone is happily engaged
Even if it is just napping in the shade.

Old and young, we share a moment in time
Three generations of family together celebrate life
We have a picnic every summer at the park
We play and have fun from morning 'til dark.

THE MAGIC OF MOVIES

How they move us, and how they thrill us
How they draw tears or make our hearts flutter
They make us laugh, they make us cry
Sometimes they make us feel invincible
They inspire us
They delight us
They even frighten us
When the scenes are too realistic.

Watching charismatic stars
With surround sound on giant screens
We are filled with awe at the special effects
And the daring action scenes
Gazing at sci-fi, horror, and suspense
Westerns, musicals or love stories
I like nothing better than an epic blockbuster
A wonderful drama or comedy.

Lois and Clark
Fred Astaire and Ginger Rogers
Bogey and Bacall
Liz and Richard Burton
Doris Day and Cary Grant
And a host of others
We've loved them all
They are the wonderful stars
That grace the silver screen
Their performances entertain us, inspire us
Make us think
And sometimes fulfill our dreams
Such is the mystery
the power
and the magic
of movies.

MY GARDEN

I look out at my balcony
And see a wave of colour
Pink, gold, mauve, yellow, red and green
It looks like a crowd of friends and loved ones
Waving gaily to me as they move
To and fro in the wind.

Their beauty soothes my senses
Their sweet fragrance appeases my soul
I feel happy to be alive
And in their presence.

And then I wonder
Why I never grew flowers before.

MY PLATONIC FRIEND

We have barely met again
it's been such a long time
since we were teens
And now we seem to have
so much to say
so much to be shared
Words come tumbling out in an eloquent rush
one after another in a hurry to be heard
You "get me" and I "get you"
you listen, and you actually hear me
It is as if I have known you
for many lifetimes
I am not afraid
to share anything with you.

That seems so strange
because in reality
you are still a stranger to me.
I find you fascinating
and am so sorry you suffered
but you have risen above it all
and you have triumphed way above and
beyond your heartbreak and pain
I feel so happy
and almost proud of you
for your successes.
I would introduce you to a lovely woman
with a heart of gold
because beautiful souls like you
should find happiness again.

I am contentedly married
perhaps not as happily as in days gone by
He doesn't quite get me
or he just takes me for granted
For me now there is not the raging passion
as once there was
Broken promises and inconsideration
have taken their toll
But there is respect
understanding and tolerance
and a liking for each other still
after all these years
Duty binds me to him
marriage is a commitment
I revere highly.

Besides, truth be told
he is a very good man with a heart of gold
If absence makes the heart grow fonder
and familiarity breeds contempt
then he and I need
to put some distance between us
Then we need to be less familiar
with each other
We work, play and live
together as a couple
He means well
is always full of good intentions
It is surprising that we still
get along so well
it almost defies reason.

Then the memories come flooding in
to remind me of the good life
we have built together
our children and the fun times
laughter and happiness along the way
The experiences we shared and
the vows we pledged to each other

You have come to me as a new friend
yet it seems that we have met
a lifetime before
I cannot cut through
the silken threads of fascination
You have me enmeshed in your gentle ways
and yes, I am captivated
I am reeling with this unexpected find
this unexpected treasure
and hope that we can share everything
except forbidden pleasure
Can we like one another and remain only friends?
Am I asking the impossible?
Can I resist your charms to the end?
The answer comes to me unbidden
and I know I must
I need to uphold my family honour
and all the bonds of trust.

ACCUSTOMED TO YOU

When I think of you and I see your face
I know I have found my home, my place
I am so accustomed to you, my love
I know you are a blessing to me from above.

I am so attuned, I spot you in a crowd anywhere
Your handsome, noble bearing—unique and rare
When you are close by and near to me
I feel your presence intuitively.

I know your heart is good and true
I know the total essence of you
I know the depth of your soul
I know you make me whole.

I know all your hopes it seems
I know every one of your dreams
I know what makes you smile
I know all the things you find worthwhile.

It seems that I know you through and through
Because, my darling, I am so accustomed to you
We are bound to each other for life
I will always be your lover, forever your wife.

YOU KNOW ME WELL

When we are together
No words are required
Your look, your smile, your touch
And the glint in your eyes tell me so much
You know me in all of my moods, in all of my phases
You've seen me at my worst, yet that never erases
Your undying love for me, nor my undying love for you
Darling, you know me well, through and through.

Without a single word spoken
Our bonds of communication are never broken
You know when I want you to hold my hand
When I need you to forgive and understand
When I want you to make love to me
Or just hold me in your arms tenderly.
My sweet, you know me well—so you know it is true
All I need to be happy in this life—is you.

GOOD NEIGHBOUR

You are kind and considerate
To live close to you is really great
Good neighbours like you are rare and few
You really do unto others as you'd have them do unto you.

You always lend a helping hand
You reach out to your fellow man
You offer an attentive ear
And always show how much you care.

Mankind can learn a lesson or two
From a great neighbour just as you
Civility in our community is what you're about
You are generous and genuine, of that there's no doubt.

It is a nice surprise to discover you shovelled my walkway
And also the pile of snow from my four-car driveway
And learning that you do this for other neighbours too
Makes me appreciate a kind neighbour like you.

Your parents and family have taught you well
You have had a good upbringing, we all can tell
You are a good person and I hope I will be
As good a neighbour as you are to me.

For Don and Stephanie Taggart and Gail Henry.

HIGH HEELS

Teetering, tottering
Flailing and fluttering
I run around in my precious heels
I think I look taller, I think I look great
Thinking little of the pain these heels create.

My chest sticks out with pride
My buttocks, rounded and accentuated
I am instantly graceful, taller and sleeker
These stilettos dictate my posture and pose
But is it really only an illusion as with *la vie en rose?*

My calves start to cramp from walking on my toes
I remove my shoes and see the corns on my soles
Not to mention the bunions that have arose
Caused by those precarious high heels that I adore.
I declare then, I will not wear high heels anymore!

FIGHT

Fight the good fight
Fight with all of your heart and all of your might
Keep your spirits up and your loved ones near
That will give you the strength to fight and endure
The battle will be tough; the battle will be long
You need support of loved ones to keep strong
Never mind the wounds and scars along the way
For sure, pain will be inflicted before we can say
We have fought long and well
We have stories of valour to tell
The rest of the world must rise to fight
Let evil never win; for evil is a blight
Upon our world and it must be eradicated
Yes! Evil must be obliterated.

So, fight the good fight for all mankind
Let not the peacekeepers be left behind
Strive for a safe world for the children's sake
Freedom and justice are at stake
In the end, the terror and violence of guns
With flowers and candles we will overcome
We must stand strong and upright
We must be united in the good fight
Against the loss of goodness and humanity
Through acts of terrorism, wickedness and depravity
My heart cries out to those who mourn and wail
Peace, flowers and candles must prevail!

In remembrance of the victims of the Paris massacre on November 13, 2015.

PERFECT LIFE

This life isn't perfect
But this life is mine
Mine to make the best of
Mine to appreciate every single day
Mine to improve at every step
And in each and every way.

My love isn't perfect
But this love is mine
My dearest holds my body, my heart and my soul
He is my true mate who makes me whole
I adore him with every fiber of my being
With him, my imperfect life is worth living.

Reclaiming my Heritage

RECLAIMING MY HERITAGE

I grew up a Chinese child, learning to speak my mother tongue at Grandma's knee and with Mama's love enveloping me. As a typical good, well-behaved child who loved her parents, I strived to excel in my studies so as to make my folks proud.

I started school at the age of four. As I was exposed to the English language being spoken all the time (at home where we ran a grocery store, and in school), it took its toll on me and I lost my mother tongue, nearly, but not completely. All that remained was a smattering of home-used words like "dinner's ready," "call your dad to eat," "pass the salt," or simple phrases and words. I could not speak a complete complex sentence, never mind carry on a conversation in Chinese.

In 1969, my family moved to Canada and a whole new world opened up for us. There was a Chinatown in Toronto, where I was exposed to more than just a handful of Chinese people. In fact, there were thousands of Chinese in Toronto. Chinese was spoken, read and written by many. Everyone seemed to be proud of their heritage and tried to retain their culture as well as assimilate into Canadian society.

I was determined to reclaim my heritage. I watched Chinese movies and luckily, Bruce Lee Kung-Fu movies were then all the rage. I listened to Chinese pop songs and could sing them, phonetically correct, but had no clue as to what the songs meant. Then, I took a Chinese class at summer school and when I started dating, I only dated Chinese boys.

I married one of those Chinese boys. My in-laws couldn't speak English and I was determined to be a good, loving wife and daughter-in-law, so I studied Chinese once again with the help of my husband and his family.

A very proud moment for me was when my father would introduce me to his friends, acquaintances and family as his fourth daughter. He would say with fatherly love: *kui doo sik gong tong wah*, which translated meant "she knows how to speak Chinese."

My crowning moment in this heritage reclamation journey was when I travelled to Hong Kong and China for the first time in 1994. I could understand and converse with ease in my mother tongue and I remember being proud of myself and feeling so happy during my first trip to the Orient. I am so pleased and proud to be Chinese-Canadian and to have reclaimed my heritage.

CPSIA information can be obtained
at www.ICGtesting.com
Printed in the USA
BVHW082315111219
566313BV00008B/349/P

9 781926 926605